MACK AP SUPER-DUTY TRUCKS
1926 THROUGH 1938
PHOTO ARCHIVE

MACK AP SUPER-DUTY TRUCKS 1926 THROUGH 1938

PHOTO ARCHIVE

Photographs from the
Mack Trucks Historical Museum Archives

Edited with introduction by
Thomas E. Warth

Iconografix
Photo Archive Series

Iconografix
PO Box 609
Osceola, Wisconsin 54020 USA

Library of Congress Card Number 96-76226

ISBN 1-882256-54-9

96 97 98 99 00 5 4 3 2 1

Cover design by Lou Gordon, Osceola, Wisconsin

Printed in the United States of America

US book trade distribution by Voyageur Press, Inc. (800) 888-9653

PREFACE

The histories of machines and mechanical gadgets are contained in the books, journals, correspondence, and personal papers stored in libraries and archives throughout the world. Written in tens of languages, covering thousands of subjects, the stories are recorded in millions of words.

Words are powerful. Yet, the impact of a single image, a photograph or an illustration, often relates more than dozens of pages of text. Fortunately, many of the libraries and archives that house the words also preserve the images.

In the *Photo Archive Series,* Iconografix reproduces photographs and illustrations selected from public and private collections. The images are chosen to tell a story—to capture the character of their subject. Reproduced as found, they are accompanied by the captions made available by the archive.

The Iconografix *Photo Archive Series* is dedicated to young and old alike, the enthusiast, the collector and anyone who, like us, is fascinated by "things" mechanical.

ACKNOWLEDGMENTS

The photographs appearing in this book were made available by the Mack Trucks Historical Museum. We are grateful to Colin Chisholm, Curator, for his assistance.

Mack AP Super-duty sales catalog cover, 1929.

INTRODUCTION

"Built like a Mack Truck." What a wonderful statement—one of the best descriptions you can give to a piece of equipment designed to stand up to tough conditions. Since just after the turn of the century, Mack has been turning out trucks of such a quality that the phrase has become part of our language. The first truck placed in the Smithsonian Collection was an Model AC—the venerable "Bulldog".

The Mack brothers first made their name as horse- drawn wagon builders in Brooklyn, New York in the 1800s. About 1902, they produced their first motor vehicle, a sightseeing bus powered by a 24-horsepower, four-cylinder engine. It was so successful that business grew and they looked for a new plant. Allentown, Pennsylvania was chosen and Mack Brothers Motor Car Company was established. It was here that the brothers produced their first trucks, which ranged in size from 1-1/2 tons to 5 tons. Later, larger trucks up to 7-1/2 tons were built.

By 1911, Mack were producing over 500 trucks a year and were generally recognized as the largest truck manufacturer in the country. However, this activity needed capital. The brothers agreed to join forces with the distributors of the Swiss Saurer truck and the Hewitt Company to form International Motor Company. The new company was a sufficiently large enough organization to gain support of the bankers. Growth quickened, with the manufacture of the Saurer truck under license and an increasing number of Mack and certain Hewitt models. Financial problems continued and two of the Mack brothers left the company.

During 1915, Mack decided to produce a completely new heavy-duty truck. The design included the novel approach of putting the radiator behind the engine, which led to its very distinctive sloping hood. The prototype Model AC was completed in 1916, and some 4,000 were bought by the US government for use in

Europe during World War I. Others were purchased by the British. The hood's appearance reminded the soldiers of a bulldog, hence the nickname of what was to become the most famous Mack model of all time. Over 40,000 Bulldogs were built between 1916 and 1938. Most came with chain drive and four-cylinder engines.

In 1926, Mack introduced a 6-cylinder engine of approximately 150 horsepower. It was initially used in Mack fire engines. As Mack saw the need for greater hauling capacity than was offered by the AC, it employed the new engine in a new heavier duty truck, the AP Super-duty. The larger engine meant an even more massive hood. Initial capacities were 7-1/2 tons to 15 tons. Most of the 285 units built between 1926 and 1938 served the heavy construction industry. Weight restrictions in most states prevented the AP from achieving high sales figures.

Most famous of the APs were those custom built for work on construction of the Hoover Dam in the early 1930s. Mack produced a special booklet extolling the contributions of the AP to the building of the Hoover, San Gabriel, and Bouquet Canyon Dams. Similar work was done by APs on the Grand Coulee Dam. The contractors showed considerable initiative by removing the dump truck bodies from the chassis and fitting concrete moving equipment and in one case a double decker bus body, after the rock and dirt hauling parts of the contracts were completed.

Mack AP Super-duty Trucks 1926 through 1938 Photo Archive presents photographs from the Mack Trucks Historical Museum. The photos appear in roughly chronological order. Where possible, we give the negative number. The four specification sheets reproduced at the end of the book will be of interest. Two of these are dated but the date of the remaining two is unknown. Very limited information was found with much of the material. The images speak for themselves, however, and we hope the reader will be encouraged into further research.

February 1929. (A2458)

March 1929. (A3138)

April 1929. (L3253)

Model AP for Champlain Refining Co., Oklahoma City, June 1929. (L3974)

March 1930. (L4328)

November 1929. (L3976)

16

November 1929. (L3979)

Right-hand drive chassis for export, December 1929. (A3727)

18

December 1929. (A3731)

Right-hand drive chassis for export, December 1929. (A3729)

December 1929. (A3730)

Winch chassis, March 1930. (A3960)

March 1930. (A3962)

Owner: Continental Oil Company
Chassis Model: AP
Wheelbase: 191 inches
Type Cab: Mack closed
Special Chassis Equipment:

Type Body:
Body Builder:
Body Dimensions:
Trailer Make:
Trailer Tire Size:
Frame Length:
Size of Body:
Special Trailer Equipment:
Miscellaneous Information:

Point Operating: Ponca City, Oklahoma
Drive: Chain Ratio: 9:26
Frame Length: 180 inches
Tires: Front, 40x8; Rear, 42x9 dual
Westinghouse air brakes, Monarch air horn, Blackmer rotary pump model 6W with Sarco strainer
Tank
Davis Welding & Manufacturing Co.
1500 gallons
Fruehauf 7-1/2 ton special
38x7 duals
18 feet
2500 gallons
Air Brakes
Gross Weight truck loaded: 25,000 lbs.
Gross Weight trailer loaded: 28,000 lbs.

This unit hauls from refinery at Ponca City to bulk plants located on paved highways within a radius of 75 miles. It is competing with an average freight rate of $.0085 per gallon, and the unit is paying for itself every year.

May 1930. (L4789) *See description on page 24.*

April 1931. (L5422)

May 1931. (L5471)

Boulder Dam chassis, November 1931. (A4883)

November 1931. (A4882)

Dual reduction drive (not chain driven) chassis for Atlantic Refining Co., December 1931. (A4907)

December 1931. (A4909)

Dual reduction drive chassis for Atlantic Refining Co., December 1931. (A4911)

Auxiliary gas tank for Atlantic Refining truck, December 1931. (A4914)

Trailer hook up for Atlantic Refining truck, December 1931. (A4913)

186-inch wheelbase Boulder Dam trucks for Six Companies, Inc., 1932. (1013)

Owner: Six Companies, Inc. (Boulder Dam Contractors)
Chassis Model: AP Dump Chassis; numbers 6AP1C1006, 6AP1C1007
Wheelbase: 180 inches
Type Cab: Mack open
Chassis Equipment: Reinforced inside and fishplated
Spoke wheels; 11.25x24 Firestone ANS 12-ply tires, front,
40x10 and 40x12 Firestone solids, single-flanged, rear
Four-wheel Westinghouse air brakes
Factory overloads
Stromberg carburetor
12-tooth front sprockets
Dual ignition with Bosch magneto
L.N. starting and lighting system
Winslow air cleaner
Zenith fuel pump
Power take-off for hoist
Steel hoods and steel guards over radiators
Type Body: Dump, No. 6 Underbody, hoist mounted
Body Builder: Heil

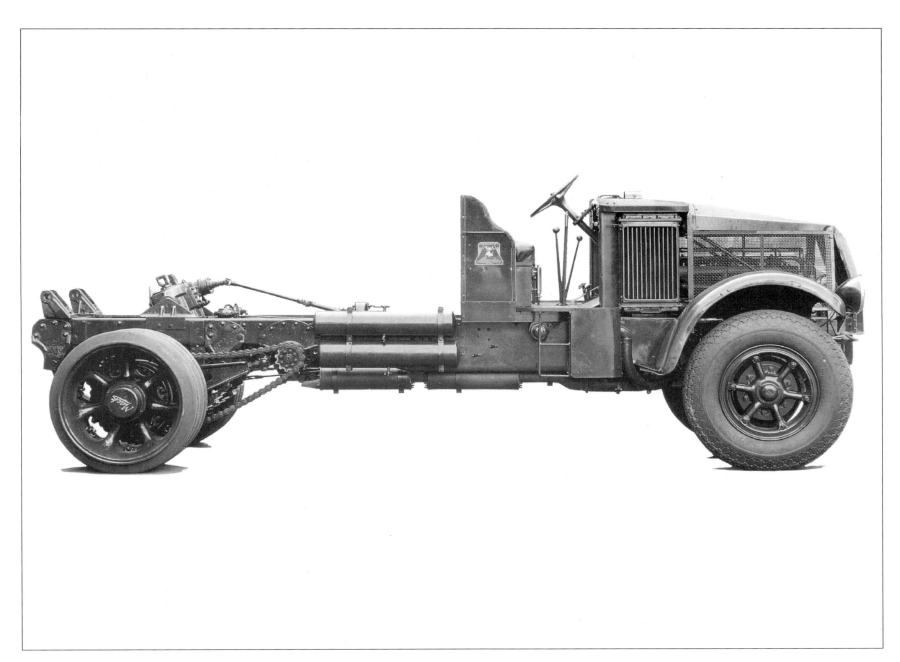

December 1931. (1001) *See description page 36.*

February 1932. (L5843)

February 1932. (L5844)

February 1932. (A4978)

February 1932. (A4979)

One of 15 chassis for Atlantic Refining, March 1932. (L5866)

March 1932. (L5865)

Boulder Dam truck for Six Companies, Inc., March 1932. (L5867)

March 1932. (L5868)

March 1932. (L5871)

Chassis for Boulder Dam truck, April 1932. (A5043)

48

April 1932. (A5044)

Chassis for Boulder Dam truck, April 1932. (A5045)

50

April 1932. (A5046)

Chassis for Boulder Dam truck, April 1932. (A5047)

Delivered October 1931. (L5772)

Dual reduction drive dump truck, April 1932. (A5025)

April 1932. (A5026)

Dual reduction drive dump truck, April 1932. (A5027)

56

April 1932. (A5028)

Six Companies, Inc. Boulder Dam trucks delivered April and May 1932. (1026)

April 1932. (1034)

Six Companies Inc. Boulder Dam trucks, 1932. (1036)

1932. (1037)

Model T-44 Woods hydraulic hoist, as used on West Slope trucks, 1932. (1060)

1932. (1061)

Boulder Dam truck hauling up to 16 cubic yards with "bathtub" style rock body, 1932. (1069)

Brown & Camillo truck at work on San Gabriel Dam No. 1, 1932. (1058)

Super-Duty Macks Triumph*

1933 is a year of building! In some sections, vast enterprises are already under way. Particularly is this true of the Pacific Slope.

Boulder Dam, the largest concrete structure in the world, has begun to take form. San Gabriel Dam, No. 1, in Los Angeles County, California, the world's largest rock fill has been started. Bouquet Canyon Dam, also in Los Angeles County, a type of structure as different from the other two as they are from each other and also one of the world's largest of its kind, is about two-thirds complete...

... the three projects have one factor common to each and to all. Motor trucks are meeting the requirements of transportation. The world's biggest dams have brought into being the world's biggest trucks. It was fitting and proper that Mack, builder of the first motor trucks in America, should continue to be first. Products of emergency requirements, yes, but products of evolution as well.

*From the 1933 Mack publication *Super-Duty Macks Triumph on World's Greatest Construction Projects*

West Slope Construction Company trucks at work on San Gabriel Dam No. 1, 1932. (1063)

West Slope truck at work on San Gabriel Dam No. 1, 1932. (1073)

Six Companies, Inc. Boulder Dam truck, September 1932. (A5269)

Six Companies, Inc. Boulder Dam truck, September 1932. (A5267)

September 1932. (A5268)

Six Companies, Inc.
Boulder Dam truck,
September 1932. (A5265)

September 1932. (A5266)

Warner Co., Philadelphia, July 1932. (L6051)

July 1932. (L6052)

Warner Co., Philadelphia, July 1932. (L6053)

July 1932. (L6053A)

West Slope Construction Co. trucks at San Gabriel Dam No. 1, 1933.

Super-Duty Macks Triumph*

The AP Macks in service on the San Gabriel job are duplicates of those used at Boulder Dam and constitute the largest fleet of this type of equipment in the country.

To date (July 1933), the West Slope Construction Co. has purchased none but AP Mack trucks for its use in connection with building San Gabriel Dam No. 1. The Six Companies, Inc., contractors for Boulder Dam, learned after prolonged experimentation in truck hauling on that project that economy of operation depends on moving as big loads as possible every trip. The West Slope Construction Co. took advantage of that experience and on San Gabriel began where the Six Companies left off. Officials of West Slope went to Boulder Dam to inspect personally the performance of the Macks before reaching their decision as to truck purchases.

*From the 1933 Mack publication *Super-Duty Macks Triumph on World's Greatest Construction Projects*

April 1933. (M121)

Backing up with driver in crow's nest. Throttle operated with left foot, January 1934. (M369)

West Slope Construction Co. operations at San Gabriel Dam No. 1,
April 1933. (M120)

West Slope Construction Co. trucks at San Gabriel Dam No. 1, 1933.

Boulder Dam truck with 8-yard tipple bucket, November 1933. (M241)

Boulder Dam truck with concrete agitators, November 1933. (M242)

3-1/2 yard bucket loads 14-yard body. Boulder
Dam, November 1933. (M243)

16-yard body on AP truck, San Gabriel Dam No. 1, January 1934. (M371)

January 1934. (M372)

San Gabriel Dam No. 1, January 1934. (M370)

Converted dump truck carries electric-driven agitators/mixers. Boulder Dam, 1933. (M243A)

270-cubic foot Commercial Shearing & Stamping dump body dumps to left or right, March 1934. (A5897)

March 1934. (A5894)

March 1934. (A5892)

March 1934. (A5893)

March 1934. (A5895)

Dump body dumps to left or right, Chassis No. 1039. (A5900)

November 1934. (M897)

Owner: California Portland Cement Co.
Chassis Model: AP
Wheelbase: 186 inches
Type Cab: Mack open

Chassis Equipment:

Point Operating: Los Angeles, California.
Drive Chain
Frame Length: 144 inches
Tires: Front, 11.25x24 Firestone; Rear, 40x16 solid; Spoke wheels
Westinghouse air brakes
Factory overloads
Delco-Remy electrical system
Mack 7-2 transmission
Special heavy tubular type rear axle
Frame reinforcement inside; fishplating outside
Woods T-44 dual barrel-type hoist
Headlamp hoods
Heavy tow hooks, front and rear
Boiler plate protection for motor and radiator
Special teel and angle iron bumper; hood screens; drivers platform and crows nest; outboard steps; chain oilers; dual air cleaner; hand-operated air brake control

Type Body:
Body Builder:

Side Dump, 19-yard capacity
Consolidated Steel Co.

November 1934. (M900) *See description on page 102.*

November 1934. (1080)

November 1934. (M899)

Cuney-Crick jobs, Grand Coulee Dam, 1934. (Libby No. 4575)

1934. (Libby No. 4500)

Cuney-Crick jobs, Grand Coulee Dam, 1934. (Lacey, Spokane, No. 8337)

1934. (Lacey, Spokane, No. 8336)

Cuney-Crick jobs, Grand Coulee Dam, 1934. (Libby No. 4572)

1934. (Libby No. 4569)

Mack Model AP six-wheeler, one of two delivered to the Columbia Iron Mining Co. for use in mining operations at Desert Mount, Utah, shown with body in raised position. The bathtub dump bodies have a capacity of 12-1/2 yards. Items of equipment include: 12.00x24 tires, 13.50x24 dual rears; Westinghouse air brakes, including auxiliary hand valve; 7.2 transmission and flexible radius rods; a reinforced frame, channel inside, fishplate outside; and extras of the type developed at Boulder Dam, such as special motor shrouding, engine front bumper, crow's nest, outboard steps, etc.

January 1936. (M1426) *See description page 112.*

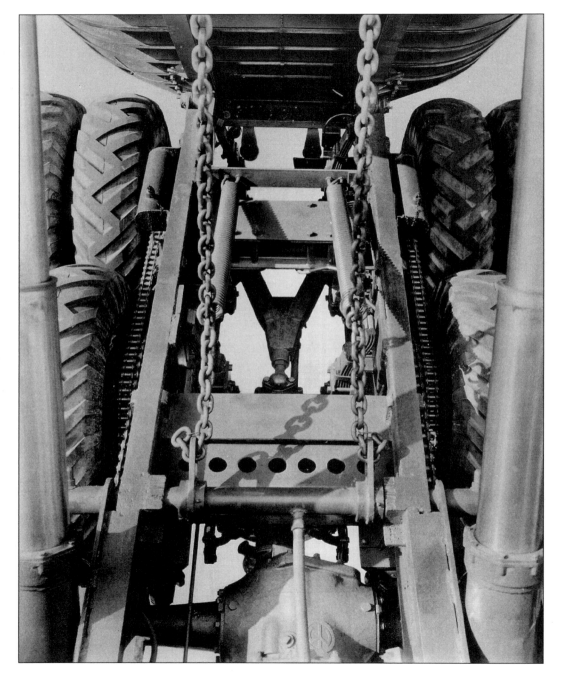

Photo page 114
View of chassis with dump body in raised position. A Model AP, chain drive six-wheeler delivered to the Columbia Iron Mining Co. This view shows the rugged, reinforced frame; double set of driving chains running from a single jackshaft; A-frame type of radius rod construction between the two rear axles; and the heavy vertical springs used to absorb the stress of sliding the tires when making a turn. January 1936. (M1424)

Photo page 115
Close up of rear of Mack Model AP, chain drive six-wheeler delivered to the Columbia Iron Mining Co. for use in hauling ore at Desert Mound, Utah. Typical of the massive rear construction of this unit are the two huge, one-piece tubular axles, largest used in truck construction. Also shown in this view is the A-frame type of radius rod construction between the rear axle and the forward axle, which provides a means of tightening the chains between the two axles and also provides for a fixed distance between the two axles at all times regardless of the action of the front radius rods which in this case are spring loaded. This view also shows the heavy vertical springs used to absorb the stress of sliding the tires while turning.(M1423)

October 1936. (M1813)

October 1936. (M1814)

Columbia Iron Mining truck. January 1936. (M1425)

April 1936. (L4625)

Circa 1946. (M9851)

BIBLIOGRAPHY

Brownell, Tom, *History of Mack Trucks*, Osceola, Motorbooks International, 1994.

Montville, John B., *Mack*, Newark, Walter Haessner, Inc., 1973.

Montville, John B., *Mack, A Living Legend of the Highway*, Tucson, Aztex Corp., 1979.

Rasmussen, Henry, *Mack, Bulldog of American Highways*, Osceola, Motorbooks International, 1987.

Mack MODEL AP 6-WHEEL TRUCK

Chain Drive

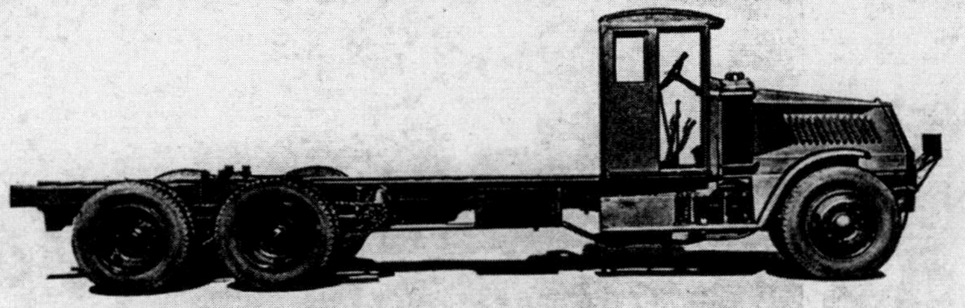

WHEELBASES 145-52", 165-52", 185-52" **SIX-CYLINDER** **150 HORSEPOWER**

THE Mack super-duty AP six-wheeler is built to handle the heaviest freighting practicable upon the highways in view of both economic and legislative limitations. Six wheels and four-rear-wheel drive permit the most efficient distribution of enormous loads to prevent destructive effect upon the roads, while a six-cylinder, 150-horsepower engine enables these immense loads to be hauled conveniently, swiftly and economically through traffic.

Exclusive Power Divider

Although the six-wheel idea has gained great popularity, it has remained for Mack, by the efficient combination of chain drive, hypoid gear jackshafts and an exclusive power dividing unit, or third differential, to eliminate the perplexing difficulties heretofore inherent in six-wheelers. Mack AP six-wheelers have proved the practicability of their type and the soundness of their construction in both private and government use.

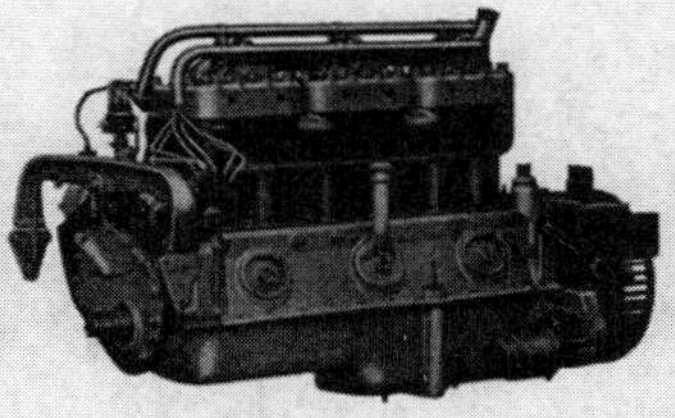

The Engine

A super-duty engine of 5" by 6" bore and stroke supplies power in abundance to meet the modern demand for speed with capacity. High compression without detonation is achieved by the use of turbulence-type offset combustion chambers, flat valves and a particularly efficient intake vaporizing device. Long life and smooth performance are insured by the largest integrally-counterweighted, drop-forged crankshaft in production, and by the perfect balance of reciprocating parts, made possible by drop-forged, machined-all-over connecting rods and a torsional vibration damper. Case-hardened timing gears, heat-treated cylinders and cold-circulation thermostatic control are other refinements.

The Transmission

A short shaft with two large universal joints extends from the dry-plate clutch to the robust four-speed transmission and jackshaft unit. The AP transmission is noteworthy for its great size, the exceptional width of generator-ground, accurately-centered gears and moderate gear reductions.

The Final Drive

Final drive is taken through two hypoid-driven jackshafts and thence through chains to the four rear wheels. The application of great power, coincident with the imposing of enormous loads, is rendered feasible, reliable and safe on the AP by the complete equalization of traction between the four rear wheels both in driving and braking; by the introduction of the third differential to protect tires and driving parts from over-stress in the event of loss of traction on one axle or in surmounting uneven road surfaces; by the assurance of traction secured by the anti-racing characteristics of the power divider. The power divider, or third differential, although absolutely essential to efficiency in four-rear-wheel drive design, is available on NO OTHER make of six-wheel truck.

The Brakes

Utmost safety is assured by powerful foot brakes acting on the four rear wheels through a vacuum booster, and by an independent disk brake. Center-point steering and a forward-mounted steering gear, precision-built, affords surprising ease of control.

MODEL AP 6-WHEEL TRUCK SPECIFICATIONS

WHEELBASES.............. 145-52", 165-52" and 185-52"
TRACK, Front.............. 71⅛"
Rear.............. 79"
TIRES, Standard, Front....... 36 x 7 solids
Rear....... 40 x 12 solids
TIRES, Pneumatic (extra)..... Optional
TURNING CIRCLE......... 54' 3" for 145-52" wheelbase
58' 4" for 165-52" wheelbase
63' 5" for 185-52" wheelbase

ENGINE—
Six-cylinder, 5" x 6"
N. A. C. C. Horsepower, 60
Brake Horsepower, 135 at 1650 r.p.m., 150 at 2000
Cylinders, Cast in block with pair-cast heads
Pistons, Invar-strutted aluminum alloy
Connecting Rods, Tubular, drop-forged. Length, 15"
Crankshaft, Heat-treated, integrally counterweighted
Main Bearings, Bronze-backed, diamond-bored, hard babbitt
Number, 4; diameter, from 3¼" to 3⅞"; total length, 11⅝"
Valves, Flat-seat, L-head at right
Ignition, Impulse starter magneto
Carburetor, 1½" duplex
Air Cleaner, Air Maze
Fuel Feed, Gravity. 40-gallon capacity tank
Governor, Centrifugal, 1650 r.p.m.
Cooling, Centrifugal pump
Thermostat, Cold circulation type
Radiator, Continuous-finned, tubular, in dash cowl
Shutters, Vertical
Water Capacity, 18½ gallons
Lubrication, Force feed and splash
Oil Filter, H.W. Filtrator
Oil Capacity, 5 gallons

CLUTCH, Mack single, dry plate type

TRANSMISSION, Selective, four speeds forward, one reverse
Location, Unit with jackshaft
Splineshaft, Interrupted type
Bearings, 8
Ratios: First speed, 6.42; second, 3.35; third, 1.80; fourth, direct; reverse, 7.66

JACKSHAFT DRIVE—
Hypoid through special splineshaft and splined flanges

FINAL DRIVE—
Through two hypoid-driven, semi-floating jackshafts and thence through chains to the four rear wheels
Universal Joints, 4
Oil Capacity, including transmission, 6 gallons; rear jackshaft, 1½ gallons

THIRD DIFFERENTIAL—
Type, Compensator, eccentric internal gears
Location, Rear of forward jackshaft
Drive, Floating shaft from transmission through hollow jackshaft pinion quill

REAR AXLES, I-beam
Road Clearance, 18⅛"

GEAR RATIOS, Optional Standards

Sprockets.....	13x41	13x45	16x41	16x45	17x41	17x45
Ratios.......	9.26	10.14	7.50	8.23	7.06	7.75
Speed, m.p.h. at 1650 r.p.m......	21.3	19.4	26.2	23.9	27.8	26.2

BRAKES—
Foot, on four rear wheels, vacuum booster actuated
Size, 20" x 3¼" each set; area, 574 square inches
Hand, On driveshaft between 2 jackshafts
Size, 16" diameter disk; 4 shoes, area 122 square inches
Total Braking Area, 696 square inches

FRAME, Heat-treated steel, flexible channel type
Size, 8" x 3"; ⅜" thick; 8 cross-members

FRONT AXLE, Drop-forged reversed Elliot with center-point steering
Road Clearance, 9⅞"

STEERING GEAR, Worm and sector with eccentric sector adjustment
Ratio, 16 to 1; 20" steering wheel

WHEELS, Steel Castings

SPRINGS—
Front, 46" x 3½"; rear, both axles, 52" x 4"
Helper Springs, 2, on cross-members direct with axles

The standard A P 6-wheel chassis also includes painting in lead-varnish (Mack green); cowl (no seat); hub-odometer, engine temperature indicator on instrument board, side lamps, dash and tail lamps, electric horn, tool box with tools, electric starting and lighting system.

Standard chassis extras include covered, year 'round, narrow or DeLuxe cab; windshield with hand-operated wiper for covered cab; electric or vacuum operated windshield wiper; bumper, government pintle hook and drawbar; dash odometer, flush type speedometer, rear view mirror, extended muffler tail-pipe, searchlight, air brakes, Mack power takeoff, 2 forward-speed auxiliary transmission, power divider or third differential.

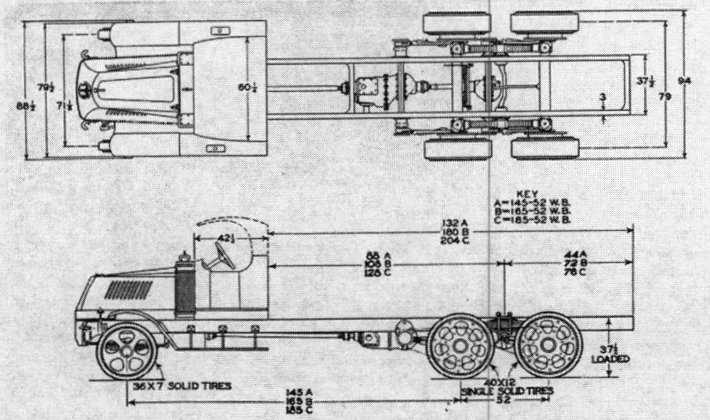

There being no annual or series models of MACK products, refinements and improvements are effected whenever sound development and thorough trial prove them to be advantageous. The right is therefore reserved to change specifications or prices without notice.

Mack MODEL AP TRACTOR

Chain Drive

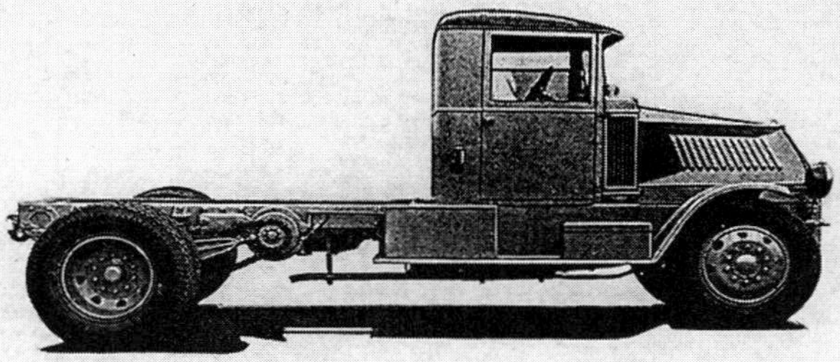

WHEELBASE 147" **SIX-CYLINDER** 138 **HORSEPOWER**

RESPONDING to the insistent demands of operators for more capacity at greater speeds, Mack has built and engineered the Mack Model AP tractor to handle the heaviest semi-trailers and trailer-trains. Although its wheelbase is somewhat longer than the conventional tractor, only a trifling increase in turning radius is necessitated, while its abundant power permits hauling of the heaviest loads regardless of grades and with gratifying acceleration ability in traffic.

The Engine

Developing a maximum of 138 horsepower, the six-cylinder engine, of 5" by 6" bore and stroke, is thrifty, smooth in operation and responsive. Despite the relatively large bore, the compression is high yet the engine does not detonate when using ordinary fuels. This is due to turbulence-type offset combustion chambers, flat valves and a particularly efficient intake vaporizing device, whereby a dry gas is delivered under all conditions without excessive preheating. Close regulation of engine temperature which is vital to efficient and economical operation in a high compression engine, is achieved automatically by cold-circulation thermostatic control. Long life and smooth operation are safeguarded by the largest integrally-counterweighted drop-forged crankshaft in production, running on 3½-inch diamond-bored bearings. Smoothness is further enhanced by the perfect balance of reciprocating parts, made possible by the drop-forged, machined-all-over tubular connecting rods and augmented by a torsional vibration damper.

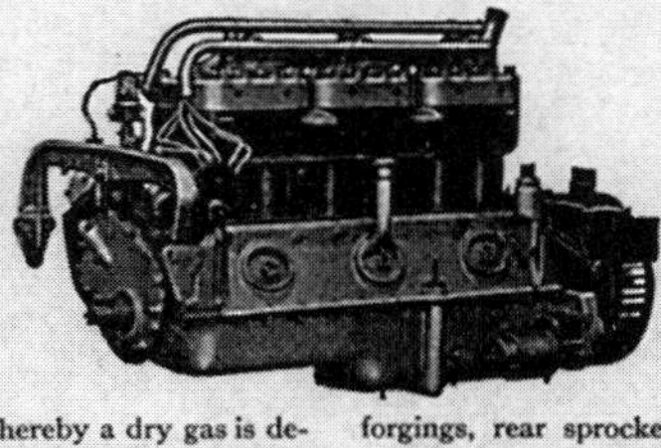

The Transmission

Drive is particularly compact, a short shaft with two large-sized universal joints extending from the dry-plate clutch to the robust four-speed transmission and jackshaft unit. The AP transmission is noteworthy for its great size, the exceptional width of its gears, and the use of the exclusive Mack interrupted splineshaft, whereon gears are accurately centered and guided. The engine's high torque permits moderate gear reductions, which mean increased life of driving members.

The Final Drive

Final drive is by side chains, which not only provide the greatest efficiency and flexibility under heavy draft but facilitate change of ratios through a wide selection and allow a particularly low mounting of the fifth wheel. Front sprockets are case-hardened drop-forgings, rear sprockets are massive steel castings.

The Brakes

Foot brakes of enormous size, acting on the rear wheels through the powerful, trouble-free vacuum booster, and a hand brake entirely separate on the jackshaft ends, assure utmost safety at any speed. Center-point steering and the use of a forward-mounted steering gear, precision-built and affording adequate leverage, results in ease of control, even under the heaviest loads.

A massive, heat-treated steel frame and long, wide and many-leaved springs, augmented by progressive-type helper springs of unusual size and capacity, absorb shocks and reduce vibration to a minimum.

Sheet 38

MODEL AP TRACTOR SPECIFICATIONS

WHEELBASE........................ 147"
TRACK, Front........................ 78⅝"
Rear........................ 75¼"
TIRES, Standard, Front.................. 36 x 7 solids
Rear................ 40 x 8 dual solids
TIRES, Pneumatic (extra) optional
TURNING CIRCLE.................. 68' 2"
ENGINE— AP
Six-cylinder, 5" x 6"
Brake Horsepower, 133 at 1650 r.p.m., 138 at 1900
Cylinders, Cast in block with pair cast heads
Pistons, Invar-strutted aluminum alloy
Connecting Rods, Tubular, drop-forged. Length, 15"
Crankshaft, Heat-treated, integrally counterweighted
Main Bearings, Four; diameter, 3¼" to 3⅞"; total length, 11⅝"; bronze-backed, diamond-bored, hard babbitt
Valves, Flat-seat, L-head at right
Ignition, Impulse starter magneto
Carburetor, 1½" duplex; throttle-actuated, graduated-heat vaporizer
Air Cleaner, Air Maze
Fuel Feed, Gravity. 40-gallon tank steel cab, 39 coupe
Governor, Centrifugal, 1650 r.p.m.
Cooling, Centrifugal pump
Thermostat, Cold circulation type
Radiator, Continuous-finned, tubular, in dash cowl
Shutters, Vertical, hand-operated
Water Capacity, 27½ gallons
Lubrication, Force feed and splash
Oil Filter, H. W. Filtrator
Oil Capacity, 5 gallons (including filter)

CLUTCH, Mack single, dry plate type
TRANSMISSION, Four-speed selective, unit with jackshaft
Splineshaft, Interrupted type; eight bearings
Ratios: First speed, 6.42; second, 3.35; third, 1.80; fourth, direct; reverse, 7.66
DRIVE—Side chain type
Universal Joints, 2
Side Chains, 1⅛" x 1¾"; pitch, 2"
Jackshaft, Semi-floating type, unit with gearbox
Oil Capacity, including transmission, 6 gallons
REAR AXLE, Drop-forged, I-beam type
GEAR RATIOS AND SPEEDS, Optional
Ratios.................Choice of 24 from 6.46:1 to 12.92:1
Speeds, m.p.h. at 1650 r.p.m. with standard tires.................From 15.1 to 30.2
BRAKES—
Foot, on rear wheels, vacuum booster actuated
Size, 20" x 3½"; area, 284 square inches
Hand, Contracting on jackshaft ends
Size, 15" x 3"; area, 194 square inches
Total Braking Area, 478 square inches
FRAME, Heat-treated steel, flexible channel type
Size, 8" x 3"; ⅜" thick; cross-members, 4 channel, 1 cast steel control, 2 drop-forged engine supports
FRONT AXLE, Reversed Elliot type, center-point steering
STEERING GEAR, Worm and nut
Ratio, Variable, 27.48:1 to 36.98:1; 20" steering wheel
WHEELS, Hollow spoked steel castings
SPRINGS—
Front, 46⅞" x 3½"; rear, 52" x 4"
Helper Springs, 36" x 4"

THE STANDARD AP TRACTOR CHASSIS also includes painting in lead-varnish (Mack green); cowl (no seat); hub-odometer, engine temperature indicator on instrument board, electric starting and lighting system, headlamps, combination stop and tail light, electric horn, tool box with tools, tow hooks front and rear.

STANDARD CHASSIS EXTRAS include covered cab with windshield or coupe cab, both with automatically operated windshield and rear view mirror; bumper, dash odometer, flush type speedometer, searchlight, air brakes, Mack power takeoff, 7-2 transmission, 7 forward speeds and 2 reverse; vacuum booster or air brake semi-trailer connection.

There being no annual or series models of MACK products, refinements and improvements are effected whenever sound development and thorough trial prove them to be advantageous. The right is therefore reserved to change specifications or prices without notice.

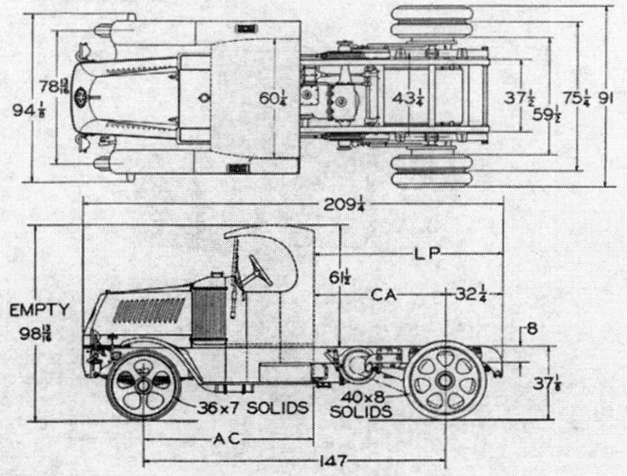

AC
Front Axle to Back of Cab
82⅛ steel cab
89½ coupe cab

LP
Load Platform Length
97⅛ steel cab
89¾ coupe cab

CA
Cab to Rear Axle
64⅞ steel cab
57½ coupe cab

Mack MODEL AP 6-WHEEL TRUCK

Dual Reduction Drive

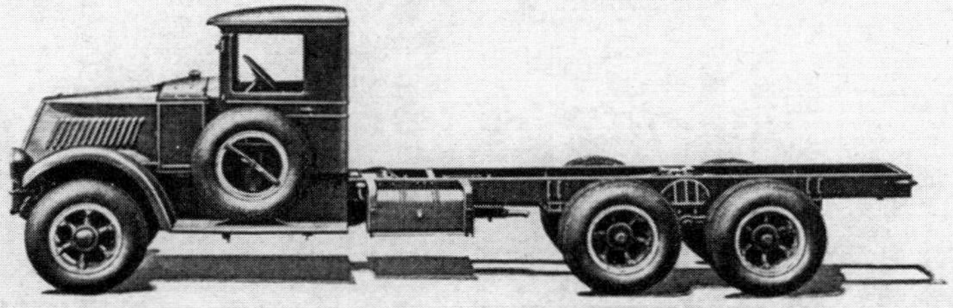

WHEELBASES 152-52", 165-52", 185-52", 205-52" **SIX-CYLINDER** 138 **HORSEPOWER**

EXTENDING the practicable fields of application of super-duty Mack six-wheelers of the most powerful type and largest capacity, to those operations in which peculiarities of soil or particular importance of silence render chain drive less desirable, a Dual Reduction drive Model AP Six-wheeler is offered.

Positive Traction

This model employs virtually identical construction to that of the chain-driven type, except for the rear axle unit. This, being of the inclosed shaft-driven type, is silent and clean. Although somewhat above the chain-driven model in weight, it has the same characteristics respecting flexibility or adaptability to uneven surfaces, positive traction and equalization of traction between the two rear axles. Spring suspension is also similar and has been so arranged that overall width is held within legal limits with the largest tires.

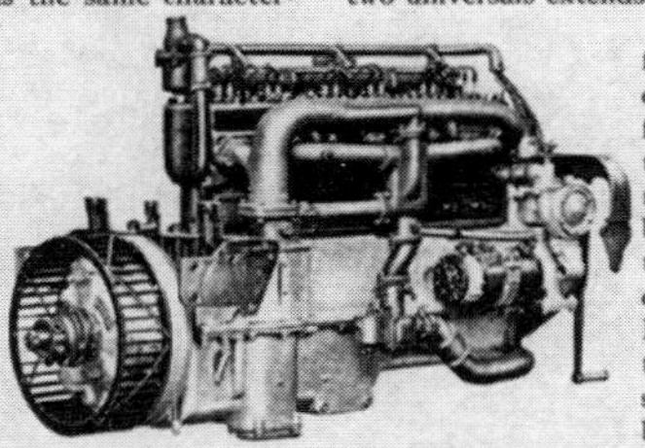

The Engine

Power for the most arduous service is supplied by the six-cylinder, 5" by 6" engine whose power output is intensified by high compression, secured without detonation by a graduated-heat intake vaporizer, flat-seat, L-head valves with renewable, Mack Alloy exhaust valve seats, and turbulence-type, offset combustion chambers. In consequence of the perfect balance of reciprocating parts, involving connecting rods machined all over, the largest integrally counterweighted heat-treated crankshaft in production and a torsional vibration damper, this giant engine operates smoothly, accelerates rapidly and withstands many years of continued punishment. Among other factors contributing to these benefits are heat-treated cylinders, case-hardened timing gears, generator-ground by an exclusive Mack process, and combination full pressure and splash lubrication. Cooling is controlled by a cold-circulation thermostat and is effected by a massive cowl type radiator with a beltless, squirrel-cage blower.

The Transmission

Drive is taken through a single plate dry clutch and a primary shaft with two universals to the four-speed transmission, independently mounted amidships. From thence a secondary driveshaft with two universals extends to the forward rear axle.

The Final Drive

Both axles are of the full-floating type, Dual Reduction driven, with one-piece, drop-forged, heat-treated chrome-nickel steel banjo housings. The drive is taken straight through from one to the other, the exclusive Mack compensator dividing the drive between the two axles so that inequalities of speed as between them, due to road unevenness or differences in the wear or inflation of tires, do not cause scuffing. Its non-spinning characteristics, furthermore, assure traction even when one axle loses it. Driving torque is taken by horizontal torque rods, acting through rubber cushions, while brake torque and propulsion are taken by radius rods.

The Brakes

Foot brakes are mechanical, air-actuated and act on all six wheels, affording utmost effectiveness and enormous wearing surface. The hand parking brake, of the disk type and acting on the driveshaft, also combines great effectiveness with unusual durability.

Sheet 22

MODEL AP SIX-WHEEL SPECIFICATIONS

WHEELBASES............ 152-52", 165-52", 185-52", 205-52"
TRACK.................. Front, 78⅝"; rear, 72"
TIRES, Standard, Front... 9.75-22 Balloon, 12-ply
Rear.... 9.75-22 Dual Balloon, 12-ply
TURNING CIRCLE...... 66'10" for 152-52" W. B., 70'11" for 165-52" W. B., 76' for 185-52" W. B., 80'1" for 205-52" W. B

ENGINE— AP
Six-cylinder, 5" x 6"
Brake Horsepower, 133 at 1650 r.p.m., 138 at 1900
Cylinders, Cast in block with pair-cast heads
Pistons, Invar-strutted aluminum alloy
Connecting Rods, Tubular, drop-forged. Length, 15"
Crankshaft, Heat-treated, integrally counterweighted
Main Bearings, Four; diameter, 3¼" to 3⅞"; total length, 11⅝"; bronze-backed, diamond-bored, hard babbitt
Valves, Flat-seat, L-head at right
Ignition, Impulse starter magneto
Carburetor, 1½" duplex; throttle-actuated, graduated-heat vaporizer
Air Cleaner, Air Maze
Fuel Feed, Gravity. 40-gallon tank; 41-gallon auxiliary
Governor, Centrifugal, 1650 r.p.m.
Cooling, Centrifugal pump
Thermostat, Cold circulation type
Radiator, Continuous-finned, tubular, in dash cowl
Shutters, Vertical, hand-operated
Water Capacity, 27½ gallons
Lubrication, Force feed and splash
Oil Filter, H. W. Filtrator
Oil Capacity, 5 gallons (including filter)

CLUTCH, Mack dry, single plate type

TRANSMISSION, Four-speed selective, located amidships
Splineshaft, Interrupted type; eight bearings
Ratios: First speed, 6.42; second, 3.35; third, 1.80; fourth, direct; reverse, 7.66

FINAL DRIVE—Through two spiral-bevel, Dual Reduction axles
Universal Joints, 5; 1 Mack Torque Insulator

POWER DIVIDER—
Type, Mack concentric cam and plunger
Location, Assembled to front of forward rear axle
Drive—Input, Direct from driveshaft
Forward rear axle, Direct from rear differential cam to bevel pinion through hollow quill
Back rear axle, From forward differential cam through shaft floating in quill to rear driveshaft

REAR AXLES, Full-floating type
Construction, One-piece, drop-forged banjo design
Oil Capacity, 2 gallons each axle

REAR AXLE RATIOS, Optional Standards

Ratios....................	6.52	7.46	8.73	10.31
Speed, m.p.h. at 1650 r.p.m. with standard tires..............	30.0	26.1	22.3	18.9

BRAKES—Foot brakes are air on all six wheels
Foot, Front, 18" x 3"; area, 192 sq. in.
Rear, 17¼" x 6"; area, 852 sq. in.
Hand, Contracting on driveshaft
Size, 15" diameter; 4 shoes; area, 88 sq. in.
Total Braking Area, 1132 sq. in.

FRAME, Heat-treated, pressed steel channel type
Size, 8⅜" x 3"; thickness, ⅜"; ¼" plate outside reinforcement; cross-members, 4 channel, 1 tubular, 1 cast-steel control, 2 drop-forged engine supports

FRONT AXLE, Drop-forged I-beam; reversed Elliot type with center-point steering

STEERING GEAR, Worm and nut
Ratio, Variable, 27.48:1 to 36.98:1; 20" steering wheel

WHEELS, Hollow spoked steel castings

SPRINGS—
Front, 48" x 3½"; rear, 52" x 4"
Helper, 22¾" x 4"

THE STANDARD AP SIX-WHEEL CHASSIS also includes painting in lead-varnish; cowl (no seat); spare rim and tire carrier; engine temperature indicator; electric starting and lighting system, headlamps, combination stop and tail light; electric horn, speedometer, tool box with tools, tow hooks.

STANDARD CHASSIS EXTRAS include covered cab with windshield or coupe cab, both with automatic windshield wiper and rear view mirror; front bumper, government pintle hook and drawbar; Mack power takeoff; 7-2 transmission, air brake trailer connection.

There being no annual or series models of MACK products, refinements and improvements are effected whenever sound development and thorough trial prove them to be advantageous. The right is therefore reserved to change specifications or prices without notice.

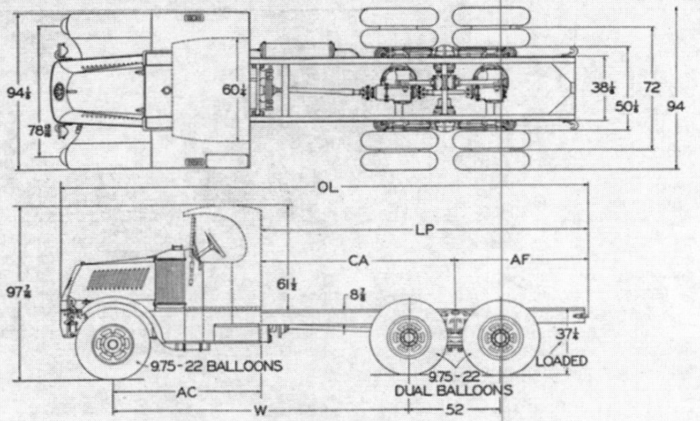

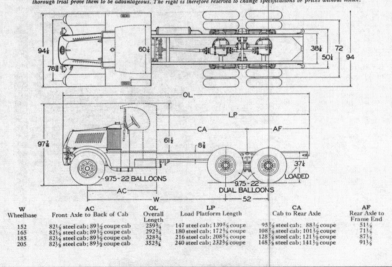

W Wheelbase	AC Front Axle to Back of Cab	OL Overall Length	LP Load Platform Length	CA Cab to Rear Axle	AF Rear Axle to Frame End
152	82⅛ steel cab; 89½ coupe cab	259¾	147 steel cab; 139⅝ coupe	95⅞ steel cab; 88½ coupe	51⅛
165	82⅛ steel cab; 89½ coupe cab	292¾	180 steel cab; 172⅝ coupe	108⅞ steel cab; 101½ coupe	71⅛
185	82⅛ steel cab; 89½ coupe cab	328¾	216 steel cab; 208⅝ coupe	128⅞ steel cab; 121½ coupe	87⅛
205	82⅛ steel cab; 89½ coupe cab	352¾	240 steel cab; 232⅝ coupe	148⅞ steel cab; 141½ coupe	91⅛

Mack MODEL AP

Chain Drive

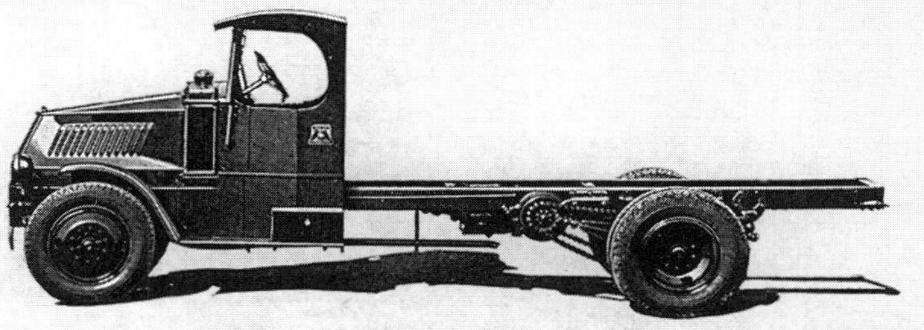

WHEELBASE 191" **SIX-CYLINDER** **150 HORSEPOWER**

SUPER-DUTY characteristics have been incorporated in the Mack Model AP truck chassis whereby maximum loads, both carried and trailed, may be moved over the highways expeditiously, legally and economically. Built upon chassis of redoubtable robustness, powered with a high-efficiency 150-horsepower engine and provided with driving parts, brake equipment and controls especially adapted to the most arduous services, these trucks follow consistently the established characteristics of heavy-duty Mack chassis. The AP has no equal for low cost transportation when there is sufficient tonnage to take advantage of big-unit economy.

The Engine

Pulling power and speed in abundance are given this model by a six-cylinder, high compression engine of 5 x 6 bore and stroke; a massive, integrally-counterweighted crankshaft and the same type of turbulence combustion chambers, flat-seat valves, efficient intake vaporizer, crankcase ventilation and cold-circulation thermostatic water temperature control as characterize all other Mack engines. Drop-forged, machined-all-over connecting rods; case-hardened timing gears and an unusually large camshaft assure unsurpassed durability and performance. An effective lubrication system is a further deterrent to wear. Model AP, like models AK and AC, employs the massive dash-type radiator and beltless squirrel-cage blower which so greatly increase cooling capacity and engine accessibility. An air cleaner and oil filter are other characteristic refinements.

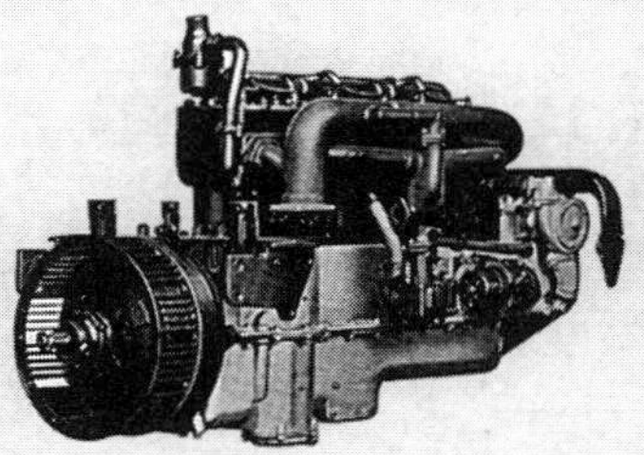

The Transmission

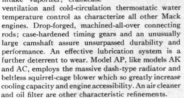

The AP four-speed transmission is noteworthy not only for its great size and the exceptional width of its gears, but also for the use of the exclusive Mack interrupted splineshaft, whereon gears are accurately centered and guided. The high torque of the engine permits the use of moderate gear reductions with consequent increased life of driving members.

The Final Drive

Final drive is by chain and sprocket, advantages of which in heavy going are higher flexibility and smoother application of power in starting the super-duty loads carried by the AP; the ease of changing gear ratios as loads and operating conditions vary, and the ease of maintenance springing from its accessibility. Front sprockets are case-hardened drop-forgings, while the rear are massive steel castings, almost indestructible because of their size. Friction losses are unusually low.

The Brakes

Utmost safety is assured by foot brakes of great size, acting on the rear wheels through the powerful, trouble-free vacuum booster, and by a hand brake which acts upon the jackshaft ends. Steering this big unit is accomplished with surprising ease by virtue of center-point steering knuckles and a forward-mounted steering gear of large size, precise action and adequate ratio.

Driver Comfort

The frame is a massive structure of heat-treated steel supported on long, wide and many-leaved springs, providing great load capacity, superior strength, utmost flexibility, maximum driver comfort and load protection.

MODEL AP SPECIFICATIONS

WHEELBASE .... 191"
TRACK, Front .... 71⅛"
Rear .... 75½"
TIRES, Standard, Front .... 36 x 7 solids
Rear .... 40 x 8 dual solids
TIRES, Pneumatic (extra) optional
TURNING CIRCLE .... 28' 6"
ENGINE—
Six-cylinder, 5" x 6"
N.A.C.C. Horsepower, 60
Brake Horsepower, 135 at 1650 r.p.m., 150 at 2000
Cylinders, Cast in block with pair-cast heads
Pistons, Invar-strutted aluminum alloy
Connecting Rods, Tubular, drop-forged. Length, 15"
Crankshaft, Heat-treated, integrally counterweighted
Main Bearings, Bronze-backed, diamond-bored, hard babbitt
Number, 4; diameter, 3¼" to 3⅞"; total length, 11⅝"
Valves, Flat-seat, L-head at right
Ignition, Impulse starter magneto
Carburetor, 1½" duplex
Air Cleaner, Air Maze
Fuel Feed, Gravity. 40-gallon capacity tank
Governor, Centrifugal, 1650 r.p.m.
Cooling, Centrifugal pump
Thermostat, Cold circulation type
Radiator, Continuous-finned, tubular, in dash cowl
Shutters, Vertical
Water Capacity, 18½ gallons
Lubrication, Force feed and splash
Oil Filter, H. W. Filtrator
Oil Capacity, 5 gallons

CLUTCH, Mack single, dry plate type
TRANSMISSION, Selective, four speeds forward, one reverse
Location, Unit with jackshaft
Splineshaft, Interrupted type
Bearings, 8
Ratios: First speed, 6.42; second, 3.35; third, 1.80; fourth, direct; reverse, 7.66
DRIVE—Chain type
Universal Joints, 2
Side Chains, 1⅛" x 1¼"; pitch, 2"
Jackshaft, Semi-floating type, unit with gearbox
Oil Capacity, including transmission, 6 gallons
REAR AXLE, I-beam type
Road Clearance, 18"
BRAKES—
Foot, on rear wheels, vacuum booster actuated
Size, 20" x 3½"; area, 287 square inches
Hand, Contracting on jackshaft ends
Size, 14½" x 3"; area, 193½ square inches
Total Braking Area, 480½ square inches
FRAME, Heat-treated steel, flexible channel type
Size, 8" x 3"; ⅜" thick; 6 cross-members
FRONT AXLE, Reversed Elliot type, center-point steering
Road Clearance, 9⅜"
STEERING GEAR, Worm and sector with eccentric sector adjustment
Ratio, 16 to 1; 20" steering wheel
WHEELS, Electric steel castings
SPRINGS—
Front, 46" x 3½"; rear, 52" x 4"
Helper Springs (extra), 36" x 4"

GEAR RATIOS, Optional standards

Sprockets	12 x 36	12 x 39	12 x 43	13 x 36	13 x 39	13 x 43	14 x 36	14 x 39	14 x 43
Ratios	6.69	10.50	11.58	8.95	9.59	10.69	8.31	9.00	9.93
**Speed*	20.6	19.1	17.3	22.5	20.6	18.9	24.2	22.3	20.4
Sprockets	15 x 36	15 x 39	15 x 43	16 x 36	16 x 39	16 x 43	18 x 36	18 x 39	18 x 43
Ratios	7.75	8.40	9.26	7.26	7.88	8.69	6.46	7.00	7.71
**Speed*	25.8	23.8	21.8	27.5	25.4	23.2	31.0	28.7	26.2

**M.P.H. at 1650 r.p.m. with specified solid tires.*

The standard AP chassis also includes painting in lead-varnish (Mack green); cowl (no seat); hub-odometer, engine temperature indicator on instrument board, side lamps, dash and tail lamps, electric horn, tool box with tools, electric starting and lighting system.

Standard chassis extras include covered, year 'round, narrow or De Luxe cab; windshield with hand-operated wiper for covered cab; electric or vacuum operated windshield wiper; bumper, government pintle hook and drawbar; dash odometer, flush type speedometer, rear view mirror, extended muffler tail-pipe, searchlight, air brakes, Mack power takeoff, two-forward-speed auxiliary transmission, 7-2 transmission, 7 forward speeds and 2 reverse.

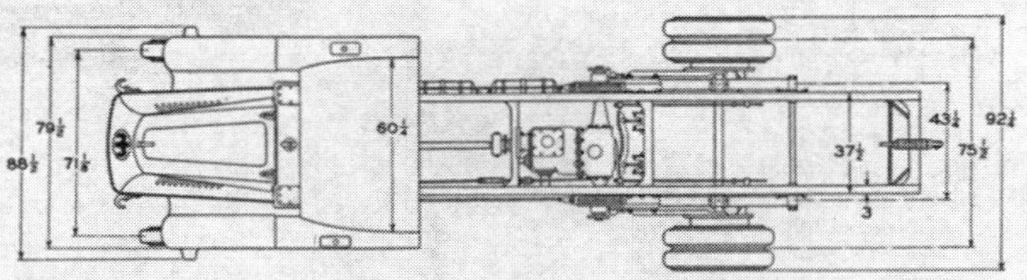

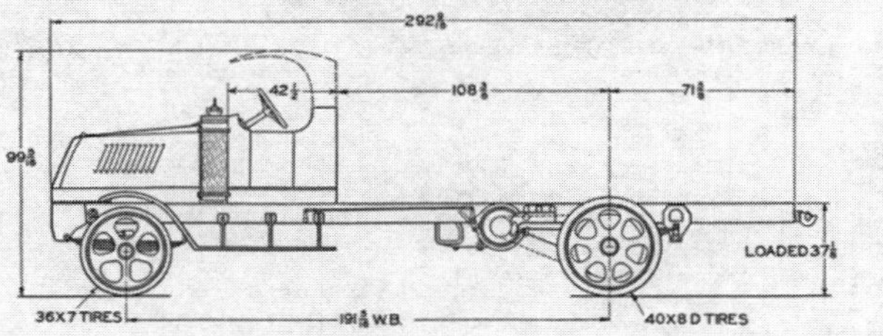

There being no annual or series models of MACK products, refinements and improvements are effected whenever sound development and thorough trial prove them to be advantageous. The right is therefore reserved to change specifications or prices without notice.

MORE GREAT MACK BOOKS

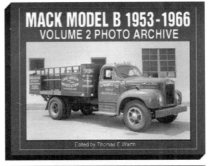

MACK MODEL B 1953-1966
Volume 1 Photo Archive *
125 rare B&W photos selected from the Mack Museum Archives. The B was one of the most outstanding & memorable of the more modern Mack models & many are still at work today. The striking rounded contours of the cab made it distinctive & relatively streamlined for its time. Soft, 144 Pgs. 11" x 8 1/2". ISBN 1-88-2256-19-0

MACK MODEL B 1953-1966
Volume 2 Photo Archive *
All new B&W photos from the Mack Museum Archives. More of the great Mack B photos that you have asked for. Like Volume 1, this book shows the Mack B in use, in a wide variety of body configurations and paint schemes. Soft, 128 Pgs. 10 1/4" x 8 1/2". 120 B&W Photos. ISBN 1-88-2256-34-4

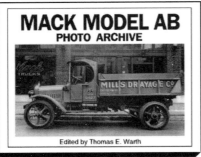

MACK MODEL AB
Photo Archive *
125 rare B&W photos selected from the Mack Museum Archives. Over 50,000 of the "Baby Mack" were produced between 1914 & 1936. Versions from the earliest prototype are illustrated in a range of applications. The restorer will find a wide variety of body configurations & paint schemes, as well as engine & chassis detail. Photos show styling & engineering development. Soft, 144 Pgs. 11" x 8 1/2". ISBN 1-88-2256-18-2

MACK® FG-FH-FJ-FK-FN-FP-FT-FW
1937-1950 Photo Archive *
Rare B&W photos selected from the Mack Trucks Historical Museum Archives. The featured trucks were the chain driven heavy-duty Mack trucks used mainly in the construction industry, both before & after World War II. Although only 1700 were built, Mack enthusiasts will find this book very attractive. Soft, 128 Pgs. 10 1/4" x 8 1/2". 120 B&W Photos. ISBN 1-88-2256-35-2

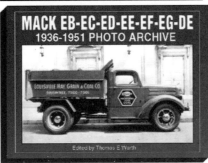

MACK EB-EC-ED-EE-EF-EG-DE
1936-1951 Photo Archive *
125 rare B&W photos from the Mack Trucks Historical Museum Archives. The featured trucks were the light & medium-duty models in the Mack E range, approximately 37,000 of which were built. Traffic-type (cab-over-engine) & conventional trucks are depicted with a variety of bodies & paint schemes. This is a book that will fascinate every truck enthusiast. Soft, 144 Pgs. 11" x 8 1/2". ISBN 1-88-2256-29-8

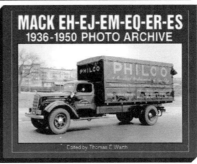

MACK EH-EJ-EM-EQ-ER-ES
1936-1950 Photo Archive *
Rare B&W photos selected from the Mack Trucks Historical Museum Archives. These popular medium duty trucks were the first Macks to have a relatively streamlined appearance. Nearly 45,000 of these trucks were manufactured. Soft, 128 Pgs. 10 1/4" x 8 1/2". 120 B&W Photos. ISBN 1-88-2256-39-5

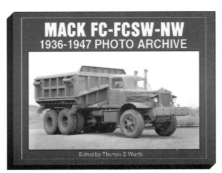

MACK FC-FCSW-NW
1936-1947 Photo Archive *
125 rare B&W photos from the Mack Trucks Historical Museum Archives. Built to order for mining & construction companies, the huge chain-driven super-duty models depicted here replaced the venerable Mack Bulldog. A MUST for every truck & construction equipment enthusiast. Soft, 144 Pgs. 11" x 8 1/2". ISBN 1-88-2256-28-X

MACK LF-LH-LJ-LM-LT
1940-1956 Photo Archive *
Rare B&W photos selected from the Mack Trucks Historical Museum Archives. These heavy-duty Mack trucks were initially developed as highway tractors. Later models were developed for the logging & mining industries. Over 31,000 of these trucks were built. This book will appeal to the logging enthusiast as well as the Mack enthusiast. Soft, 128 Pgs. 10 1/4" x 8 1/2". 120 B&W Photos. ISBN 1-88-2256-38-7

The Iconografix Photo Archive Series includes:

AMERICAN CULTURE

AMERICAN SERVICE STATIONS 1935-1943	ISBN 1-882256-27-1
COCA-COLA: A HISTORY IN PHOTOGRAPHS 1930-1969	ISBN 1-882256-46-8
COCA-COLA: ITS VEHICLES IN PHOTOGRAPHS 1930-1969	ISBN 1-882256-47-6
PHILLIPS 66 1945-1954	ISBN 1-882256-42-5

AUTOMOTIVE

IMPERIAL 1955-1963	ISBN 1-882256-22-0
IMPERIAL 1964-1968	ISBN 1-882256-23-9
LE MANS 1950: THE BRIGGS CUNNINGHAM CAMPAIGN	ISBN 1-882256-21-2
PACKARD MOTOR CARS 1935-1942	ISBN 1-882256-44-1
PACKARD MOTOR CARS 1946-1958	ISBN 1-882256-45-X
SEBRING 12-HOUR RACE 1970	ISBN 1-882256-20-4
STUDEBAKER 1933-1942	ISBN 1-882256-24-7
STUDEBAKER 1946-1958	ISBN 1-882256-25-5
LINCOLN MOTOR CARS 1920-1942	ISBN 1-882256-57-3
LINCOLN MOTOR CARS 1946-1960	ISBN 1-882256-58-1
MG 1945-1964	ISBN 1-882256-52-2
MG 1965-1980	ISBN 1-882256-53-0

TRACTORS AND CONSTRUCTION EQUIPMENT

CASE TRACTORS 1912-1959	ISBN 1-882256-32-8
CATERPILLAR MILITARY TRACTORS VOLUME 1	ISBN 1-882256-16-6
CATERPILLAR MILITARY TRACTORS VOLUME 2	ISBN 1-882256-17-4
CATERPILLAR SIXTY	ISBN 1-882256-05-0
CATERPILLAR THIRTY	ISBN 1-882256-04-2
CLETRAC AND OLIVER CRAWLERS	ISBN 1-882256-43-3
FARMALL F-SERIES	ISBN 1-882256-02-6
FARMALL MODEL H	ISBN 1-882256-03-4
FARMALL MODEL M	ISBN 1-882256-15-8
FARMALL REGULAR	ISBN 1-882256-14-X
FARMALL SUPER SERIES	ISBN 1-882256-49-2
FORDSON 1917-1928	ISBN 1-882256-33-6
HART-PARR	ISBN 1-882256-08-5
HOLT TRACTORS	ISBN 1-882256-10-7
INTERNATIONAL TRACTRACTOR	ISBN 1-882256-48-4
JOHN DEERE MODEL A	ISBN 1-882256-12-3
JOHN DEERE MODEL B	ISBN 1-882256-01-8
JOHN DEERE MODEL D	ISBN 1-882256-00-X
JOHN DEERE 30 SERIES	ISBN 1-882256-13-1
MINNEAPOLIS-MOLINE U-SERIES	ISBN 1-882256-07-7
OLIVER TRACTORS	ISBN 1-882256-09-3
RUSSELL GRADERS	ISBN 1-882256-11-5
TWIN CITY TRACTOR	ISBN 1-882256-06-9

RAILWAYS

GREAT NORTHERN RAILWAY 1945-1970	ISBN 1-882256-56-5
MILWAUKEE ROAD 1850-1960	ISBN 1-882256-61-1

TRUCKS

BEVERAGE TRUCKS 1910-1975	ISBN 1-882256-60-3
BROCKWAY TRUCKS 1948-1961	ISBN 1-882256-55-7
DODGE TRUCKS 1929-1947	ISBN 1-882256-36-0
DODGE TRUCKS 1948-1960	ISBN 1-882256-37-9
LOGGING TRUCKS 1915-1970	ISBN 1-882256-59-X
MACK MODEL AB	ISBN 1-882256-18-2
MACK AP SUPER DUTY TRKS 1926-1938	ISBN 1-882256-54-9
MACK MODEL B 1953-1966 VOLUME 1	ISBN 1-882256-19-0
MACK MODEL B 1953-1966 VOLUME 2	ISBN 1-882256-34-4
MACK EB-EC-ED-EE-EF-EG-DE 1936-1951	ISBN 1-882256-29-8
MACK EH-EJ-EM-EQ-ER-ES 1936-1950	ISBN 1-882256-39-5
MACK FC-FCSW-NW 1936-1947	ISBN 1-882256-28-X
MACK FG-FH-FJ-FK-FN-FP-FT-FW 1937-1950	ISBN 1-882256-35-2
MACK LF-LH-LJ-LM-LT 1940-1956	ISBN 1-882256-38-7
STUDEBAKER TRUCKS 1927-1940	ISBN 1-882256-40-9
STUDEBAKER TRUCKS 1941-1964	ISBN 1-882256-41-7

The Iconografix Photo Archive Series is available from direct mail specialty book dealers and bookstores worldwide, or can be ordered from the publisher. For additional information or to add your name to our mailing list contact:

Iconografix
PO Box 609/BK
Osceola, Wisconsin 54020 USA

Telephone: (715) 294-2792
(800) 289-3504 (USA)
Fax: (715) 294-3414

US book trade distribution by Voyageur Press, Inc., PO Box 338, Stillwater, Minnesota 55082 (800) 888-9653
European distribution by Midland Publishing Limited, 24 The Hollow, Earl Shilton, Leicester LE9 7N1 England

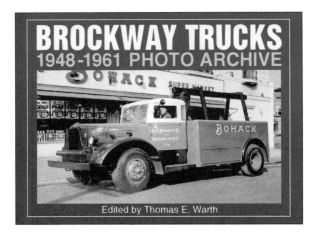

BROCKWAY TRUCKS
1948-1961 PHOTO ARCHIVE
Edited by Thomas E. Warth

MORE
GREAT BOOKS FROM
ICONOGRAFIX

LOGGING TRUCKS
1915-1970 PHOTO ARCHIVE
Donald F. Wood

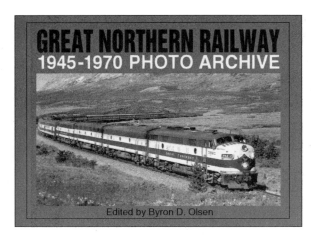

GREAT NORTHERN RAILWAY
1945-1970 PHOTO ARCHIVE
Edited by Byron D. Olsen

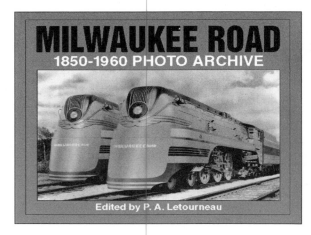

MILWAUKEE ROAD
1850-1960 PHOTO ARCHIVE
Edited by P. A. Letourneau

BEVERAGE TRUCKS
1910-1975 PHOTO ARCHIVE
Donald F. Wood

Coca-Cola
ITS VEHICLES IN PHOTOGRAPHS 1930-1969
Howard Applegate

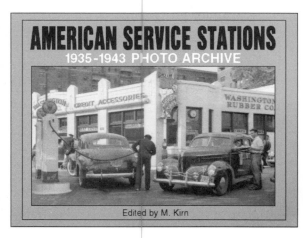

AMERICAN SERVICE STATIONS
1935-1943 PHOTO ARCHIVE
Edited by M. Kirn